W9-DFE-521

# The Measure of Islands

Other books by Mark Halperin

*Backroads*

*The White Coverlet* (chapbook)

*Gomer* (chapbook)

*A Place Made Fast*

# The Measure of Islands

## Mark Halperin

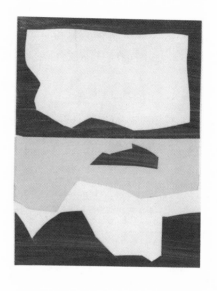

Wesleyan University Press
Middletown, Connecticut

Some of these poems appeared originally in *The Chowder Review, Crab Creek Review, Crazyhorse, Denver Quarterly, Kentucky Poetry Review, The Montana Review, The New Jersey Poetry Review, The New York Poetry Journal, Panoply, Poetry Now, Prairie Schooner, The Seattle Review, Skyline, Telescope, Tendril, Willow Springs*.

The author was aided in completing this manuscript by a Faculty Research Grant for which he is grateful to Central Washington University. He thanks Philip Garrison and Joseph Powell for their help.

The art in this book is by Bobbie Halperin.

All inquiries and permissions requests should be addressed to the Publisher, Wesleyan University Press, 110 Mt. Vernon Street, Middletown, Connecticut 06457

LIBRARY OF CONGRESS CATALOGING-IN-PUBLICATION DATA

Halperin, Mark, 1940–
    The measure of islands / Mark Halperin. — 1st ed.
        p.    cm. — (Wesleyan poetry)
    ISBN 0-8195-2177-9 — ISBN 0-8195-1179-X (pbk.)
    I. Title.    II. Series.
PS3558.A396M43    1990                                    89-36079
811'.54—dc20                                                   CIP

Manufactured in the United States of America

FIRST EDITION

WESLEYAN POETRY

# Contents

I

# Snowfall

Something stalks Father in his lair
of drawers and cubbies. Dahlias in albums,
Russian vowels—a subterranean
troll's down there. Mother drums

on the neat table upstairs and smokes.
The children draw on a steamed window:
oval, two dots for eyes, a slash
mouth to eat the feathery snow

falling about the house. The heart
starts like a snowfall remembering.
But there's no face for the loneliness
that follows, no richness to bargain

with the ditch where sighs and remorse
drift in fog, only a bodiless
fear that falls through the future
held off with promise after promise.

# Walter Benjamin, the End of Summer, Marseille

He has turned Klee's *Angelus Novous*
into an emblem about to move away
although the image could as easily advance.
Still, the angel is all potential,
jaw and wings stressed, and will sprint
into some intractable event. This too
Benjamin twists into privacy
until only he can see the O of its mouth.

Thus the New Angel becomes the Angel
of History, its eye on events
that collapse into a single oncoming
catastrophe, piling wreckage
on wreckage. And though the angel
would repair the damage, unable to furl
its wings, it is driven into the future
backwards. Its feathering hides

the mountain of debris and, behind that,
Paradise, from which the storm blows.
In Marseille, Benjamin must lift the painting
from its packing case in Paris where
it is raining. He has every reason
to believe he will cross the frontier
and depart for Portugal and New York—
visa, ticket, currency—all in order

to escape the new order of history's
self-proclaimed ally. A Roman tower
guards the harbor entrance, breaks rain
slanting in from the Mediterranean.
Coffee, the rocking lights of trawlers,
German spoken with a compatriot
he has luckily met in the street and brought
to this table. Perhaps his luck has changed

and the fine editions and paperweights,
minutiae he collected to own, parts of
himself, have been abandoned temporarily.
The gleam of the streets hardly resembles
Paris or the internment camps where
the French held him. For K
he shows off his latest collection,
a dozen white pills should he be captured.

Far too many, he says, spilling out half
for his friend. Benjamin doesn't believe
luck changes, but the time hasn't come
to forgo that pretense. He can project
an essay in which the Angel, a messenger,
circumvents the wind he called "progress."
*On the subversive nature of endings,*
he titles it, under no illusions.

The pills nestle next to the visa.
He pats the full pocket. Bad luck
is the last thing he will talk of to K.
He gets up, pays for both of them.
Dull, plodding murderers are after him.
The rain in its wings, light spilling
eerily across its back, an angel rushes off
as his steps ring the cobbles like dull bells.

# Goyishe Kopf

My father would climb from the basement
to smile knowingly. *Goyishe kopf,*
he'd chide at a silly question about
politics. Streetlight fringed the trees
as he buried a large hand in my hair.

"Gentile head," it means. And now
I bow mine to him uncovered,
my neck too straight for a Jew's.
For fifty years he lived next door
to Americans and never learned

to speak without an accent or
trust them. When goyim call themselves
"goys," watch out, he'd say. Father,
I heard it, and an old confusion, Jew
or gentile, foreigner or native-born

came back to me. *Goyishe kopf,*
I chided myself for you, splitting
a monologue in half. We're all goys,
Dad. Who speaks Yiddish or Hebrew
or even Russian here? But some nights

we come out into the open, Jews
on Yom Kippur, the moon's spotless
light covering our heads. Our chests
seem drums then and we beat out
the only tongue we've faith God knows.

# From Yeats

Six nights without dreams: it robbed
the waking soul and terrified.
The seventh day a girl came calling.
He told her her technique was worse
although he was *amazed at the tragic
magnificence of some fragments.*

Then she ran through pouring rain
to the shore to drown herself, half
drowned believing, and in sodden clothes
danced on the stones. In a lodging house
a swami gave her clothes and money
and in Barcelona she went mad.

He heard she'd climbed out a window,
fallen through a baker's roof
and broke her kneecap, that she'd hid
in the bowels of a ship. When he arrived
she was sitting up in bed writing
the full account of recent madness.

Sleep without dreams was death
and dreams without sleep the madness
of white gowns and lye soap. He paid
her bills. From fear of journalists
he kept the distance seemly for a man
grown old in the long nights.

Troubled by a lack of dreams,
he dreamed her: divided mind, heroic
dancing not on stones by a hungry sea
but below its surface, the ship's hold
littered with bales and baskets,
the lulled rise and fall of such breathing.

# Aunt Dunia

No one wrote you died; therefore,
it doesn't matter and there's no date—
your face flares at any periphery.

I give up on Pushkin, say, drop
the book, and there you are to explain
what I think I am, what I want to be

and who I come from, annoyed more than angry
at my puffed pride that Pasternak has won
the Nobel Prize. Why doesn't he address

the Jewish Problem? you ask, then tease,
can we just decide what we want to be?
My butchered Pushkin and poor Russian's

no missed opportunity or occasion for guilt.
Even on this tame shore, Aunt Dunia, each
life differs impossibly from any we recall.

# Astonishing Tasks

Even to the abruptness
of speech, quirks of phrasing
that would deflect his pen
from the angle of prayer, he strives
to make a full account, although that role
is best left to the Holy Spirit,

who was in Joseph when they spoke,
is in him as he writes and will be gone
when he no longer follows its dictates.

Consider all unclean, it counsels,
the Apostles stumbling over again
against a parable, thickheaded
failures as much of intelligence
as belief. It heaves like a lake
the day a wind picked up huge boats.

He'd meant to ask the older man
why he had been chosen, but spray
recalled grain, a balance in movement
of darkness over light or behind it.

These who know shall see and those who do not

also perform astonishing tasks.
The leper instructed to make his offering
and return home in silence marks
each man's failure to honor
the life that goes on without us,

and the Gentile directed to broadcast his cure:
balance in opposition. At the door
a boy is yelling his name,
dove, then boy again,

the fleeing soldiers, a patch, fleeting white,
of linen or thighs in a cave of darkness.

# Early October with Cows

Across the field, stacks of hay bales bulge
　　from the rectangle of my neighbor's,
　　propped with a jiggery of poles.
Cows that appeared by the fence one day
last spring, skittish, fly-ridden,
　　lower their eyes and go on
eating. Leaves rattle; long grasses rub

like insects' legs that hummed summer along.
　　More cows are coming, black-
　　and-white with thickening hides
and fat slobbering tongues, the afternoon's
few drowsy bees. The sun rakes leaves,
　　its low slant across the field,
red on the stacks of tottering hay. Soon

it's too cold to sit outside, too loud
　　once the crows begin to mob.
　　An owl repeats the wind, a gate
the loose click and grate of the earth
turning. The cows drift toward winter,
　　small, heavily laden ships
rolling slightly in the chop and swell.

## Dreyfus Pleads for the Lives
## of Sacco and Vanzetti

Before I knew these days, troubled
as they were, should lay down a calm
I would return to often, my thoughts
sat in the shade facing the sea.
Preoccupied, shaking with fever, they
directed my eyes over the waves, in times
of storm rising with the furious water.
Those who wrote later were right: the city
had seemed gray, a blotch most mornings,

and the children, beloved irritants,
my focus, a career as seen through pince-nez.
And for all the trials, I might have
gotten through well enough, but the island
crippled me making too plain the nature
of hope. What does it matter that we eat,
sleep or dress? Five years pass, quick
or slow, in one place as inviolably as
another. The silences are terrible.

June 6, 1897. At night, under pretense
a sailboat had been sighted, Commandant
Deniel ordered a blank cartridge fired.
I was awakened by cannon shots followed by
rifle shots. I saw the sentry, weapon
drawn, look at me—and rolled over.
Which was fortunate as his orders
were peremptory. My years were hostage
to imagination. In health or sorrow

to dwell too long on oneself rolls a stone
over the heart. Sunsets, lines of rain
become diversions that chiefly wash free
one salt, replacing another more foreign.
A tempest, gusts one after another—

the hut would tremble. When I saw
water again after two years, my eyes
refused rest. I had believed logic
rested in things and events, in human

justice as in talking, and was shocked
at the effort required to start toward
others. The island left me shrunken,
with a habit of minimizing exposures.
Still, I retain perhaps more imagination
that those two, foreigners the papers say,
Italians. I suppose the chronic poor
feel little. But those, neither fatherland
nor honor to hold to, hold to violence.

When guards would bring my ration, pork,
some rice, moist sugar, coffee berries
I had no means of roasting and which,
in bitter derision, were given me raw,
I threw all into the sea. What remorse
they prepare for themselves, I thought,
for history keeps no secrets. I intended
to wait. That is the difference. I write,
"greatest moral disaster in years," and

"it is fighting providence to commit
the irreparable when doubt exists," sign
my name, August 22, 1927, my dullness
the paradox I am not meant to solve.
Through the window I look on the sea,
waves tinged silver by moonlight
and clouds. They break at the foot of rocks,
powerless, their executioners, an outline,
always the measure of an island.

# Eclipse

What scared us that afternoon
was bruise mostly, my skin black
and blue and pleated where the snout
of the dog struck; it would fade
in days. On our morning walk,

tilting the pink pocket mirror
you'd tucked behind a swallow's nest,
you paused to show the tiny beaks
inside. Squatting beside my son,
you seemed to wait for yours.

Later, you'd call someone I found
remote, *an early adult,* and the moon
would slip into clouds. Some childhoods
drag on, friend. You suffer yourself
as a form of sincerity, fearing

a future that comes empty and too full.
By nightfall the moon had escaped,
disguised as nothing. The throbbing
in my leg, though I denied it, ran on
on slower time. *It's an eclipse,*

my son shouted. The wind sipped pines
while we drank wine. And when the moon's
scarred edge returned, we lifted our glasses—
for good-night kisses, we told the child
who slept as we went on drinking.

II

# March

The curtains hover, whitening
like sails almost able to push you
to another childhood where the past
pauses politely before entering.

It's spring, a little sister
who's unfastened all your moorings.

Your wife waits for you to finish
your last sip of coffee, for
your good-bye kiss. She could be
settling into a deep all her own.

The wind's up, chickadees swaying
the feeder. The blue flowers outside
nod to you. Even the empty bowl

gleams oddly like a boat for one.

# Lucy, Running

When some dogs remember
to look back, what's to see
  but the blur behind them
shrinking? Scents bloom, insist
  dogs are for taking down
what can't outrun them: snakes,
  mice; deer in deep snow.

What can your harsh voice
accomplish or clanging the gate
  behind her? If you succeed
you train her to be less. One day
  her head will drop. She'll
eye you, needing to knock something
  down. Now when she sleeps

she dreams of salt and her
stride lengthens till she's flying
  over the barbed wire. Your
call hangs a split second longer
  than flesh. A rifle crack
could never reach that far, nor she
  hear pleading or turn back.

# Passion

Driven by a thirst like any
that can't be slaked, you enter
a body of water, heart athud
at the lap and moist encircling.
When you cast, you watch mayflies
twitch and struggle to crack
shells both skeleton and hardened
past. You can see them caught
in the water's thickened surface,
can watch them free themselves,
draw their wings full length,
arch to dry and the slightest
breeze skim them. What could be
another's rise in flesh beyond
control isn't, precisely as one
passion is never another though
their discarded husks burn with
one light and, at a touch, one
body becomes all the world.

# Hosea

Ever since he could drape rain
over his shoulder and let it
fall like a cape into the straight
furrows, he has been listening:
a deer trying to become trees
and rocks; a lion, to catch its breath.

He heard them speak by straining
to keep still. Later, something
behind the wind bestowed a message,
but smooth as cloth across a lap.
He remembers one woman and thinks
he might have cherished her more.

The end would have been idolatry.
All worship is not the same. We move
one way. An orchard delights us.
Soon it bends in abundance. When
we separate the fruit, the branch
springs from our hands. So the heavens

open and shut. So all calls
tempt us. We heave words into
a sea of faces, watch them mill
and roil. How could we love
beyond our reach? Why do others
remain unalterably themselves?

# From Hayward Hill

While we were arguing, even as I slammed
outside because *what else is there to do,*
something must have called or calmed me.
The distant hills darken, then the flats,
the river turning in wide bends below.

When that goes black whatever's remote
or estranged weathers to a final selflessness,
without trees or stirred water. This is
land too stark for scars, dark basalts
and ashen soils looming each spring to burn

and dim. You could convince yourself
whoever lived here had to grow that way.
But the wind insists it isn't true, hissing
like the steam that drove me, screaming
*out,* until where I was wasn't a place to stay.

Then I needed a space that would pay me
no mind, a cold hill whose side I could climb
and claim a while. I drove or was driven to
this part of darkness. And when alarm drives me
again, I'll wind down, looking for lights.

# Six Dreams of Zuleika, Potiphar's Wife

I.

I have chosen a small, dusky horse,
adorned it with an egret plume, purple
and black edged and at its crest
scarlet. We trot
into the desert. When the last
house of the city has fallen
beneath the horizon, there is a house,

a garden at its center and a fountain,
water splashing on stones,
the patter so soft
I fail to hear my horse wander off.
Potiphar, who I recognize by his long,
swift strides more than any sign

of dress or feature, approaches
down a dark hall and from a distance.
How the placement of arches
resembles our house. A stone
steams on the marble floor
by my feet. I look for
the horse, desperate
to leave or lean on him,

point to him—I don't know.
In my hand the halter
shrinks, the size
I might wear, the feather
broken in my thoughtless grasp,
its tip clumped and moist.

2.
The child, large-headed, heavy
at my left breast, dangles
like a gold or amber amulet
stretching my nipple. I doze too, then
as I shift him to my right, as
he does, I smile and plunge

a long way toward that deep
satisfaction. One pale bluish
drop of milk in the corner
of his mouth. His eyes flicker
as if they would open

and I am in my bedchamber, it is
night. I hear cranes slide and flap
to a stop above the reed banks,
their poky walk stalking frogs.
The booming stops. It frightens me

less than the dark figure who has
raised himself from my bed.
Though the flicker of an oil flame
is absent, the moon edges
into the room it will soon flood
with shadows. Beneath the receding form

lies a figure, legs splayed, head
lolling. Her gown
has been tucked above her hips, her knees
raised, bent—a pearl
pendulant between those lower
lips, the smile

my smile. She has flung
her left arm out, palm up. Alongside
her exposed breast, where it folds
under the brown crescent
birthmark and mole
which are mine. I watch her sleep,
the billowing of thin curtains

through which a man has stepped.
I smell the Nile in flood,
its movement, sweep of its barges, heavy
sleep, the almost foreign
luxury of the sated.

3.
Amid trains of servants, plumed
and on horseback, they arrive, the women,
in twos and threes, or descend
from slings, arrayed in silks,
kohled eyes, the indentations of their necks
lit by opalescent pearls. We smile
greetings and move through

sudden turns, dartings so swift
our skirts flutter and behind,
our shadowed legs. Speech breaks
in short bursts like jungle birds, a flitting
of yellow, green and magenta
between the folded leaves. Above,
a rat twitches in a palm.

Oval couches, oval side tables;
I delay the meal, dally and attempt
to arouse them with myrrh, aloes,
cassia—my breasts, my pouting
stomach. A carp rises
to a bubble drifting on the surface.

About to wake, I push down like
a swimmer from that bright mirror's
gleam which contracts, expands,
finally a servant's tray, laden
with dates, a paste of almonds, goat milk,
where figs and crushed cakes float
like fingers, like poised butterflies.
On each gold plate an orange,

beside it, a sharp knife.
When they raise and pull back
their heads, the stalks of their necks
premonitions of
death's viperous, fleeting chill, I savor
an instant prepared here
and in my anticipation:

Joseph enters, his thin robe parting
like water before a prow, flaps
brushing. From the ewer of fresh wine
he spills a few drops at each stride.
As he swerves by me I say
*eat* and my guests fumble at their oranges,
raise the dripping slices
to their lips, with bloody hands.

*Bloody hands,* I shout later, after Joseph
has gone, a point upon which pleasure
and pain settle freely, the similar
screams. I tell them
Joseph walks these halls each day
like a knife
rending a pool, a golden, wriggling carp.

The weight on my chest is air's
but monstrously heavy. The feel of blood,
like oil or fluent silk.

4.
Joseph, a spider, a red pike
blazoned on his abdomen, lounges
in the dark corner by my sitting room.
Or near the front hall or linen room
where he instructs the maids
individually in the proper washing
and folding of cloth squares.
I look up to find at the other end
of a hallway, a courtyard, some telltale
motion signing a recently altered glance.

Now his steps echo
mine in the corridors; my comb,
missing two weeks, reappears. He
has found it by the riverbank,
looming above me, mouth above nose,
staring at my breasts, the tops
of my burning thighs. I enter
the kitchen to find him
drinking from my cup, tongue
slowly rounding its rim. He offers
berries from his white, blazing
palms. He must have me

as jasmine must ride the breeze
by the east wall. I
back toward him while the servants,
the other slaves, sleep, making a small cry,
to fall: the burning dark, moister
and moister air, on and on. Joseph,
I whisper, at last. The echoing
confines, the stone walls
of dripping rock—they answer

but Joseph scurries up
the one rope, the dot of his face
a hole in the brightness
above my head. My tears are prisms;
they invert. I am lost.
When I raise my hand a last time
it clenches on Joseph's coat: white
explodes into red, green, purple.
The sign of Potiphar stitched on its shoulder
flames. And I have it, have
him, though for what purpose
my loneliness cannot tell.

5.
The sacred field of punishment rolls
toward me, emerald-hard. Potiphar,
a hawk, circles. Joseph talks
with a group of Pharaoh's men.
Wind fingers the hem of my cotton shift.
Hail pelts my guards, who flee.
But, the guilty one, I must
continue by myself and arrive in time.

Joseph, a scowl riding his face, turns
away. From behind a tree, the hooded man
I had not seen steps out: thick-
shouldered, a wide leather belt.
He smells of sweat or semen or fish
flapping on the exposed deltas.
The sun burns down. Potiphar
drifts around, it. I brace.

The hooded man rips my shift
with one yank from its collar,
reaches between my shoulder blades—
it is as if I were demasked,
less pain than shame, bleeding
as women bleed. Under Joseph's stern gaze
I shrink and my Lord Potiphar the hawk
swings his loop still lower.

I swoon into blue haze and when I wake
a string of red beads or berries
enlarges at the white line scribed
on my neck. My cries break over my head.
Potiphar begins his glide. I feel

the air he sweeps, the one rough talon
that tears his mantle, the other
that guides him. Above and behind him,

looking down into my face,
Joseph amuses himself.

6.

As they pass my alcove, the guard
who steers him by the elbow
and Joseph, gaunt in a dark robe,
my eyes run over that back and flank,
still greedy. I command the guard to leave,
then a pitcher of wine, melons,

a divan. I compose my breath until it rules,
stiff and correct, that face infected with patience.
Part of me would fall to her knees in belief

but she is heavy. The decisive one
limbers a cane to cut stripes on his back
like a slave girl dancing. She
draws her gown over her knees,
the cruel curve of her mouth. A welt,
feathered poles that stir the air:

to their rise and fall I am telling
*the moon shrank as if it had grown old*
*and reptiles, knobby, yellow-eyed, crept*
*into houses of the rich, slithered beneath*
*their beds—the stink of their shriveling.*

Joseph, who steers Pharaoh through his dreams,
takes my elbow. Potiphar screams for his turn.
The echoes ring us down the narrow corridors.

III

# A Face Rises in the Kitchen Window

and because my father wanted his ashes
fed to swirls of air, the handfuls of
pebbles I might have topped his stone with
weigh me down. He must have guessed

how far, his parents a language away
tending to flowers or paring nails—
and labored to balance that equation
he knew the terms of in his despair.

In ground mist, a bridge could seem
capable of wondrous traffic, halos
at either end, and the moon clear,
a plate I slip from sudsy water,

slick with my father's face in mine.
Is this the window to throw pebbles at,
the lamp to wreathe with moths? Father,
are meeting places shining everywhere?

# Travels

Some calm, frosty morning like today's,
when I am tempted to ask where I have been,
let me recall the colorful cities, exotic
as the reds on the ground and bone-white grasses:
the blues of Migal, San Blas, Petrovoretz,
the many grays of boulevards in Barcelona,
gold lions on a bridge in Leningrad
and the pinks that dotted Jalapa's rainy terraces.
I have been further than I dared hope—

to Kiev and Marseille and Jerusalem, cities
swirled in history. That morning—
should the year drag toward an end as I divide
what I thought I chose from what I know
was imposed, luck against skill, work versus
accident—let me remember Oaxaca's market stalls
packed beside each other, red and black squares,
crammed with spices, and the tilting scales.
Or Yalta, the Black Sea's glistening, impossible

backdrop for hand-piled potatoes and stunted beets,
rows of pasty women in babushkas, expressionless
until their small scales began to sway, until
fresh puff-bread and the smells of the bakers
wreathe all they wrap and sell. Remind me of
my wife calling, at the far end of the field
an eagle perched in the top of a wintry tree,
white head and white tail, and may be all
that has been or will be stolen from eternity.

# Families

They meant us to overhear their gossip
as they worked a loose brick on the stoop,

a bit of some pulp lodged between
their teeth, but confided suicides,

failures of nerve, in corners, in tones
it took us years alone before we could

repeat. And trusted time would dull
the hunger that persists in longing—

and deftly mixed and troweled their mortar
to fix the unsuspecting into families.

# Living with a Drunk

You hardly notice how the drinking
    touches you until there's
a coolness and that's what he is,
    you not much with him, not
interested. You dust. You call

his sister. Living with a drunk
    you learn to care for
yourself. He may pay the bills,
    bring flowers home, but he's
not home. Better find a warm place

and buy it. One day, alive or dead,
    he's gone, you're old,
the kids are grown. What's to talk
    about? Like a beaten woman
who holds her arms before her face

instinctively, you learn not to stake
    too much on someone else's
attention. You visit anyone who asks
    and look away in time. Say
guests mill at the dinner party, drinking.

Maybe a fight begins and the two men
    step outside to cool off.
You naturally drift toward the kitchen.
    Women's talk and darkness
steam the windows. There's nothing

to see. When the glasses are cleared
    and you've done the crossword,
you wrap your arms around yourself
    like thin covers. You talk of
weather back home, the night's chill.

# Leah

I.
Leah has been crying for ages,
but even those wells eventually dry.
She's rubbed the fine hairs from her eyes
and her puffy lids droop now,
each a stoical pouch of grief.

Here comes Jacob, the stink
and bawling of belled sheep
as they near water,
and a girl, Leah's sister,
who appears as if a mirage
and for whom he lifts the well-cover.

Leah will believe she has escaped
her father's endless schemes
by giving up hope in a separate life.

She will think she does not have to marry
some wicked, eldest son. Sheep beat down
the grass where she lives,

lack of water shrivels the heart
and idols only speak when bathed
in blood. Leah will not see
that where none hunt, in a land
of traps and falls, she's her father's
ploy for keeping Jacob hard at work.

2.

No more surprises, she begs, recalling
how Jacob first turned to her
the morning after they were married,
the wells of his disbelief.
He'd fled the tent where she is
sweeping his footprints. Tomorrow

sister becomes sister twice over:
Rachel, who rose early, would
climb the stubby hills, only
a streamer of bright cloth between them,
and Leah would imagine

throngs of children poking the robes
of her hampers for presents
she had tucked there, a love
less obliged than a father's
or husband's—clouds of dust.

She assumed the children must be
Rachel's. It calmed her
desiccated body, smoothed
the irks that bristled from her.
Pity? What could be kinder
than this unassignable moment.

3.
Skies above Canaan abound in rain.
Lush grass waves on the hilltops
in autumn's winds. Leah is buried
under the children of her children.
She sits as if on a beach
each morning and watches them
cross wide vistas. They unfold

and then collect toward evening
to her. Sharp-eyed, curious,
her sons finger and shift
the coverings of the land. Their
strong arms uproot rocks and herbs.
Today Ruben returns with a mandrake,
holds it aloft in the encampment

then drops it like a trinket
in her ample skirts. When shadows
smudge the sharp divisions between tents
Rachel comes, having seen, desiring
the forked root. She will barter a night
with Jacob. As age exaggerates their differences,
their differences become their characters.

Wide-hipped Leah in dark robes can harden
Jacob, insinuate like a breeze shyly
flapping a tent wall. She retains
for him a measure of the exotic,
spice and fragrance. The unfamiliar
way, the pleasure she takes
undoing him—this is her power.

4.

Amid the balancing and contradictions
it is easy to lose sight of Leah. Her sons
are not the line that marks the patriarchs.
Remember Joseph? Who comes after him?
Remember Dinah? These are figures on a road
that crosses a landscape of such richness
famine must seem unlikely, time traveling
important as the shaggy trees, the altars
going up, the wells going down and the caves

that hold the generations of a family.
For Rachel the train of sheep and camels,
bearers and baggage and children halt.
Benjamin is being born, *Benoni,* "son
of misfortune," she calls him as she dies.
Oaks spot the hills, outcroppings of granite
where they bury Rachel, erect a pillar
and rejoin their journey, the story of
Edom and Egypt, Joseph and Benjamin

and an old man whose name becomes Israel.
The women are other women, the legends of
fathers swallowed by famine and a foreign land.
One more request and Jacob will draw his feet
into the bed, yielding. He asks to be buried
in the cave at Machpelah. *There they buried
Abraham and Sarah his wife; there they buried
Isaac and Rebecca his wife; and there I buried
Leah,* he says, carefully listing them in pairs.

# Shores

Last night, when the voices of lovers
rose from under a bridge, I heard steps,
the separate life each of us keeps creating.

My son reminds me, stumbling in from sleep.
His mother's paper cut-outs of Mt. Rainier
and framed homage to Hokusai remind me:

there's a bridge behind which Fuji looms,
crossing it, peasants with bundles of straw—
tiny, burdened figures the artist included

for scale. The lovers never heard. Something
flowed on, dark with all that water and
the stiff selves the stars turn childishly above.

A moment brushed their lips, demanded,
and the lovers, accepting, lay down
beside each other as shores the future joins.

# A Hummingbird for Mandelstam

Its obstinate, unhelpful desperation
annoyed me. I'd forgotten you, old man,
scooping the disheveled feathers
in a magazine, until I slipped back
the sash and bent looking into its eyes.
That started up the little motor,
got it thrashing to the opening,
its feet so frail they couldn't bear
the negligible weight, hoisted
and hovering in air. And now

like the Petersburg you're singing
from an unmarked grave, the lemon Neva
and brutal century must bind us.
What did I want so much I failed
to hear the crash against the window
inside the garage? Why did I assume
freedom lay in going back the way
it came? I remember a blur
a few feet from my face, amazed
before it took off, bruising us both—

*in the valley that rushed between*
*a liquid cooled so slowly a tap*
*could set it: crystal in eternity—*

before leaves resumed their rustling.
That bird's eyes were of such onyx
fright could plummet unobserved
with a stupor it almost dies from
every night. Above the dazed honey
of the Neva, a soul could taste
nectar of the deathless, and beyond
the tyrant's *lapas,* butterflies
and bees and hummingbirds, flights
of brief but touching happiness.

## Soutine's Two
### *Pageboy at Maxim's*'s

The reds, dark magentas in one,
come forward, less ripe in the other

but brighter than tomatoes and longing
to burn. The pointed chin, raised

brows, mouth and flapping ears—
is this the same boy in the same red

uniform? Was there ever more than one
painting? Or are these two boys

as those whose selves barely touch?
Legs akimbo, here's a doughy face

that joins the shoulders where they sag.
Here, buttons down the front blaze

then drip like tears, one by
silvered one. Someone's rounder

or slimmer. Someone's the same all right,
though his mouth, backbone and hips

tip him this sullen way then
that around the squat light.

Once he was poor. He had to sit.
A line cut out the space

between his cocked arms. Once
circles he completed he completed

resting each hand on its fingertips.
He was saturated paint, the head

and pain atop. Now he's not so flat.
He's on his feet and needs less,

sits or stands inside the scarlet,
can afford to dream he smells dinner

or separates his change, drawing it
up into two piles, tall

and slender. He can recall
his mother folding a white handkerchief

over and over, the dark
stairs he'll leave by.

# Rescuing the Past

1.

I remember the green under a stand of alder,
the thickened sunlight twisting, water
over boulders and the dappling that hid salmon.

In eddies a tail twitched. A white scar
darted upstream. Logging trucks and flatbeds
with fresh-sawn two-by-fours rumbled by.

Suppose in the fragments of all the days
I can't recall one day, the kids and I,
eyes streaming in a truck's acrid mist.

2.

And suppose my memory displaces a tree
from one bank to another—attempting
to frame the scene more aptly. Could that be

less a lie than some necessary fiction,
and the way the trucks disappeared
one more instance to recall, to join to

the current's troubled white ribbon?
Frothing, it goes on inventing itself
as we do, as the past does through us.

3.

Those children perished in a flaming house
or, as you tried to believe, escaped
to woods whose trees surround us: worlds

we were expelled from entering this one.
When I turn away now, eyes burning, an arm
flutters from a bus—another fragment joins

the rescued past. If we succeed, who knows
which are the invented memories
crossing the half-light of their forests?

*Daphne* and *Juris* and *Alexey* and *Benjamin*.

# Nightfall

Each of the birds has found a purchase
on the day, a branch, and tucked its head
in feathers. The sky's thin patches of red

spread south. My Dear, tomorrow's wind
coils in the mountains. Outside and within
the world has turned another of its bright

blank pages. Listen, the insects are humming
a space that's completed. Love's speechless:
afraid to tell its secret: the lack of news.

IV

# Lafcadio Hearn in Matsue

Perhaps all of us learn to love that which we train ourselves to make sacrifices for, whatever pain it may cause.

**HEARN**

I.

From the sixth floor
the city spreads out—yellow
  of sodium, the white
cones of street lamps and fields
  of tiny glowing windows.

Hearn's Matsue shone more dimly.
  Shoji glowed pale white
or yellow, baffling oil flames or
  flickering hooded candles.
The same stars burned, but fewer

  human lights said: others
are awake and about in their separate
  rooms, sleep's cotton on their
lips; its fog has not yet dropped
  from their shapes either.

2.

Hearn's having cold *soba,* a salad
of pickled *daikon.* There's *miso,*
rice and a small fried whitefish.
He slurps his noodles, studies plates,
bowls, the tray's design. The wind
is ruffling leaves, glazing the garden.

He nods to someone on his left,
bows to someone on his right,
managing a slice of slick squid
with the slender *ohashi*—hard
work amid the constant bending
and weaving. He tries because

it frees him from conversations
he cannot enter or eavesdrop on,
pinned already like an insect
on display. If he lets himself
he'll feel the sheer glass,
the suffocating lack of space.

He shudders then begins again,
the pink rind and white center
of the *kamaboko,* sharp points
of leaf under it, and small
rectangular plate which rises
at each edge. Now he can marvel

at his luck: globes of peonies
on one plate, blue crayfish
on another, beyond the garden,
the hills and clouds. A sharpness
like greed helps him concentrate,
the teeth of his many hungers.

### 3. DRUNK

He is listing, falling headfirst
toward a wheat field. Sudden men
have caught him under the armpits.

Righted, he starts the small cup
in the direction of his mouth, but
it slips off, right of the lips,

spilling a little. Hearn plummets
for what seems to him a long time
toward the mat. Tomorrow recriminations.

Tomorrow new luck, branching in all
directions till common shrubs seem
recompense enough for any man.

But tonight the white cup looks up
reflecting a face he only turns
obliquely toward us. Tottering drunk,

even his thoughts lurch: God's face,
the Medusa's engorged eye . . . He twists,
pushing off a dream he lunges for.

4.

When I woke, mist mounted straight up
from the moat, under it a sharp smell
of human waste that billowed to the Castle's
board and stone. Massive brown hawks
cried *rii, rii rii,* then rose and fell

looping through the rear garden,
turning by the pond, the pine, blue stones,
flutterings of cloth, at some invisible
barrier—of air or pure volition.
They spiraled higher till a view opened.

Last night, the insect singers hushed.
We listened to the cold inscribed
on the wind. The weather gathered at Hokkaido
to pay its respects. We couldn't know which
part was ours, only that it must arrive.

5.
The taxi drives a narrow alley.
Tipsy on wine and flatfoot clumsy,
I navigate the passageway. There's
a bar, a TV, a smiling woman.
Three or four men at the far end
greet us. I'm hemmed in. Bottle,
glasses, a slate which I sign.

I drink. Asked to, I sing.
Pictures of Golden Gate Bridge,
hills and cable cars. We take
turns at the microphone. The pictures
shift. I'm nudged to watch a woman
massage her erect nipples which
resemble the dark snails I eat
with a wooden pick. I sip.

The whiskey glass stays brimful.
The barmaid calls my boss. He
enters singing. Others join,
too far away to hear or call to.
A hand reaches toward me. When I
stretch to take it, I am in bed, it is
light out. I can't recall what I said.

### 6. In a Japanese Garden

The trees have been planted so that autumn
will gather in their layerings of deep
magenta, bright oranges and yellowed streaks
of red. Contrasting barks, bole and leaf-form

and branching pattern confront the time that's stable
across seasons. The trunks are remnants, shorn
or thinned to stubs as if wind gnawed them
or ages of ice left them ribbed and gnarled.

The horizon's scored: twigs, a clump of needles,
the gash in the hillside. With a trim vigor,
the sand suggests a stream, the rocks, an order

to the almost-natural scene. The stone lantern
in bent grass, combed and clipped moss—
disparities intended to be noticed.

7.

A two-quilt night: under the weight
of that wool I am surrounded
by only trapped body heat. I wake to
howling in the building's corridors.

I turn repeatedly. Morning's cloudy,
a mist on the roads, and the light
another atmosphere to run through
in sodden clothes. The streets fill

with trucks and cars. I could be
anyone at peace approaching home
and those dogs, leaping in greeting
when the fangs of vertigo sink in.

## 8. Dragging for the Dead

Hearn crosses the bridge, strains
toward a dimming Lake Shinji,
then the way the river flows
toward the invisible bay. He
is collecting: sounds of *geta*,
of steamers and Japanese words
new enough to resemble music.

Soon he'll travel south, Matsue
tremulous in memory, tentative
as dreams. Hearn can't know
he won't be leaving Japan. He
senses something simpler: Matsue
feeds him as no teacher's salary
could. He collects, needing

the money, needing his words
somewhere he has left for good.
He writes of a Jizo temple:
"bronze drags; and whenever anyone
has been drowned, the body not
recovered, these are borrowed. . . ."
Hearn is dragging a landscape.

He notes nothing of the heavy
and dull, the prim and cheerless
satisfaction recovering the dead—
only obligation: "If the body
be thus found, a new drag
must be presented to the temple,"
walking, casting, hauling in.

## 9. TAKING A BREAK

When I ask for two pieces of advice
Rainer offers: "Don't tell all you think,
and don't decide too quickly"—one
caution broken into easy halves for
a newcomer apt to be so dazzled,
he may find all differences except
his own. "Four years among the people . . .
scarcely suffices the foreigner to begin
to feel at home. . . ." Gratitude would round
Hearn's shoulders. When Imperial Japan
steamrolled into China, he would be gone,
the need for circumspection, dead—
the vicious, mean and small in him
all purged. Another man fastened
his sharp teeth into Matsue, froze
and begged to leave. When he comes
back, it's in dreams. Shinji spreads
its molten reds at sunset and it's him,
ahead of me wherever I walk, fierce
loneliness leashed like a dog at his side.

# New Man at Zen
*Manju-ji, Matsue-shi 1987*


I am trying to sit upright, count
my breaths and heel a doggish mind that trots off
   endlessly—only to end up
waiting for the priest's rounds. When the handbell,
   *rin,* ripples the air, I unfold,
climb down and join the others blindly pacing
   the hall's sunlit squares. Crows caw.

There are sparrows in the shadows or trees.
   The new man has remained cross-legged
on the platform. Wooden clapper, *hyoshigi, rin.* Adrift
   in time again, I climb back. Now
the priest's determined tread, oarlike staff
   firm in his grasp. The new man has clasped
his hands together, but so late he must wait

   for the priest's return. *Rin* to stretch,
*mokugyo* to chant to. As the ringing fades,
   we jump up. We bow, kneel quickly, touch
forehead to mat, hands beside, palms up.
   The new man's slow. Three rounds
and he's completely out of phase, rising
   when we fall, falling as we're done.

After the priest's hurried out, we roll our cushions,
   bend twice and head for cake and pickles.
I slide the tray to the new man, look back
   and it's unmoved, to the right a neighbor
handing him a cup of tea. When I leave, I see him
   stumble at the closed gate, the stick
no longer tapping. Someone is running to help.

# The Hawks of Matsue

The hawks of Matsue swim in air,
rolling left and right, tumbling
as they spiral groundward. Near
asphalt, their wings unfurl
to the very tips as they struggle

up, clearing the buildings, and soar,
pure city hawks, wind and climb,
as if with some filched treasure
of rings or scarves like pirates.
Soon they're back. They wait

hunched above the slow canals
scanning sunken tires, turtles,
clouds of fish like bubbles,
On poles or roof stanchions,
separately, they flex their talons.

One strips a still-wriggling catch,
screeches, then eats. Another, empty,
steps off into nothing, each
trusting air, daring
its wings not to bear it.

# Mists and Imagined Fields

As an eye sweeps the horizon's stubby mountains,
graying, layered blues, a wedge of lake
glinting between the tall buildings and fields
of orange roofs, how easy to imagine
this is the day we arrived: fallen leaves
and snow, the renewed green and a welcome mist.

That snaps the heat spell. A fine mist,
floating rather than falling, swathes the mountains,
serpentine as memory. We will leave
ghostlike flames behind to dance on the lake
at evening, grit to burnish it. Imagine,
clean each morning, the waiting, misty fields

scented like fresh sheets. They are paddies, not fields
though. We want only what is, like mist,
so fleeting yet full it could not be imagined:
lashed bamboo drying racks, mountains
of pine feathers, and sunsets on the lake
burned into our dreams although we leave

by intricate paths and gates. Before we leave,
the arches of the bridges should echo the field
of weeds in a graveyard taking the wind, the lake's
every curving inlet. We should have missed
nothing. But to the west, past the mountains,
is a town with fish in the streets. Who could imagine

the yellow and orange dots on their backs? Imagine
missing that. Is there time before we leave
for everything: camping in the mountains?
street festivals? the sky a field
of fireflowers, booming with blooming mists
that hang a few seconds above the lake

in puzzled brilliance? When we are gone, the lake
will return to darkness and quiet. We can imagine
all that follows as unimportant. What is missed
is lost. Familiar faces, the day we leave,
might shine from frozen photographs, from fields—
and part of us remain in the eyes of the mountains.

Trying to imagine our return, did we leave
ourselves stranded by lakes in those mountains,
waving from their bridges, dissolving like fields of mist?

## About the Author

Mark Halperin became interested in physics and in poetry while at Bard College, from which he was graduated in 1960. He became a junior research physicist, then worked as an electron-microscope technician for the Rockefeller Institute while he studied philosophy at the New School. Later, he attended the University of Iowa's Writers' Workshop, and received an M.F.A. in 1966. He has been a visiting professor of writing at the University of Arizona, an exchange professor at Shimane University, in Matsue, Japan, and is now professor of English at Central Washington University.

Halperin has published two other books of poetry, *Backroads* and *A Place Made Fast,* in addition to two chapbooks. He received the Glasscock Award in 1960 and the United States Award of the International Poetry Forum in 1975. He lives in the country outside Ellensburg, Washington, near the Yakima River.

## About the Book

*The Measure of Islands* was composed on the Mergenthaler 202 in Galliard, a contemporary rendering of a classic typeface prepared for Mergenthaler in 1978 by the British type designer Matthew Carter. The book was composed by Graphic Composition of Athens, Georgia, and designed and produced by Kachergis Book Design of Pittsboro, North Carolina.

WESLEYAN UNIVERSITY PRESS, 1990